D1037916

And to Every Beast . . .

Treasures of the Vatican Library

(Book Illustration)

And *to* Every Beast . . .

Turner Publishing, Inc.

ATLANTA

Compilation Copyright © 1994 Turner Publishing, Inc.
All rights reserved under international copyright conventions.
No part of the contents of this book may be reproduced or utilized in any form or by any means, electronic or mechanical, including photocopying, recording, or by any information storage and retrieval system, without the written consent of the publisher.

The Scripture quotations contained herein are from the New Revised Standard Version Bible, copyright © 1989 by the Division of Christian Education of the National Council of the Churches of Christ in the U.S.A., and are used by permission. All rights reserved.

The illustrations in this book are taken from Latin volume 276 in the Urbino Collection, The Vatican Library.

Published by Turner Publishing, Inc.
A Subsidiary of Turner Broadcasting System, Inc.
1050 Techwood Drive, N.W.
Atlanta, Georgia 30318

First Edition 10 9 8 7 6 5 4 3 2 1
ISBN: 1-57036-101-0

Printed in the U.S.A.

Treasures of the Vatican Library: Book Illustration

And to Every Beast . . ., a small volume in the Treasures of the Vatican Library series, offers a selection of miniature masterworks of book illustration from the collections of one of the world's greatest repositories of classical, medieval, and Renaissance culture. The Vatican Library, for six hundred years celebrated as a center of learning and a monument to the art of the book, is, nevertheless, little known to the general public, for admission to the library traditionally has been restricted to qualified scholars. Since very few outside the scholarly community have ever been privileged to examine the magnificent hand-lettered and illuminated manuscript books in the library's collections, the artwork selected for the series volumes is all the more poignant, fascinating, and appealing.

Of course, the popes had always maintained a library, but in the fifteenth century, Pope Nicholas V decided to build an edifice of unrivaled magnificence to house the papacy's growing collections—to serve the entire "court of Rome," the clerics and scholars associated with the papal palace. Pope Sixtus IV added to what Nicholas had begun, providing the library with a suite of beautifully frescoed rooms and furnishing it with heavy wooden benches, to which the precious works were actually chained. But, most significantly, like the popes who succeeded him, Sixtus added books. By 1455 the library held 1,200 volumes, and a catalogue compiled in 1481 listed 3,500, making it by far the largest collection of books in the Western world.

And the Vatican Library has kept growing: through purchase, commission, donation, and military conquest. Nor did the popes restrict themselves to ecclesiastical subjects. Bibles, theological texts, and commentaries on canon law are here in abundance, to be sure, but so are the Latin and Greek classics that placed the Vatican Library at the very heart of all Renaissance learning. Over the centuries, the library has acquired some of world's most significant collections of literary works, including the Palatine Library of Heidelberg, the Cerulli collection of Persian and Ethiopian manuscripts, the great Renaissance libraries of the Duke of Urbino and of Queen Christiana of Sweden, and the matchless seventeenth-century collections of the Barberini, the Ottoboni, and Chigi. Today the library contains over one million printed books—including eight thousand published during the first fifty years of the printing press—in addition to 150,000 manuscripts and some 100,000 prints. Assiduously collected and carefully preserved over the course of almost six hundred years, these unique works of art and knowledge, ranging from the secular to the profane, are featured in this ongoing series, Treasures of the Vatican Library, for the delectation of lovers of great books and breathtaking works of art.

"And to every beast of the earth, and to every bird of the air, and to everything that creeps on the earth, everything that has the breath of life, I have given every green plant for food." And it was so.

GENESIS 1:30

. . . every wild animal of every kind, and all domestic animals of every kind, and every creeping thing that creeps on the earth, and every bird of every kind—every bird, every winged creature. They went into the ark with Noah, two and two of all flesh in which there was the breath of life.

GENESIS 7:14–15

Every creature loves its like, and every person the neighbor. All living beings associate with their own kind, and people stick close to those like themselves. What does a wolf have in common with a lamb?

ECCLESIASTICUS 13:15–17

So out of the ground the Lord God formed every animal of the field and every bird of the air, and brought them to the man to see

what he would call them; and whatever the man called every living creature, that was its name.

GENESIS 2:19

Then the Lord God said to the woman, "What is this that you have done?" The woman said, "The serpent tricked me, and I ate."

The Lord God said to the serpent, "Because you have done this, cursed are you among all animals and among all wild creatures; upon your belly you shall go, and dust you shall eat all the days of your life."

GENESIS 3:13–14

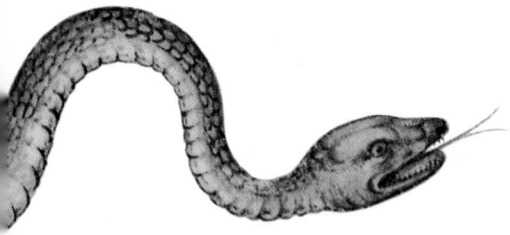

But the Lord provided a large fish to swallow up Jonah; and Jonah was in the belly of the fish three days and three nights.

JONAH 1:17

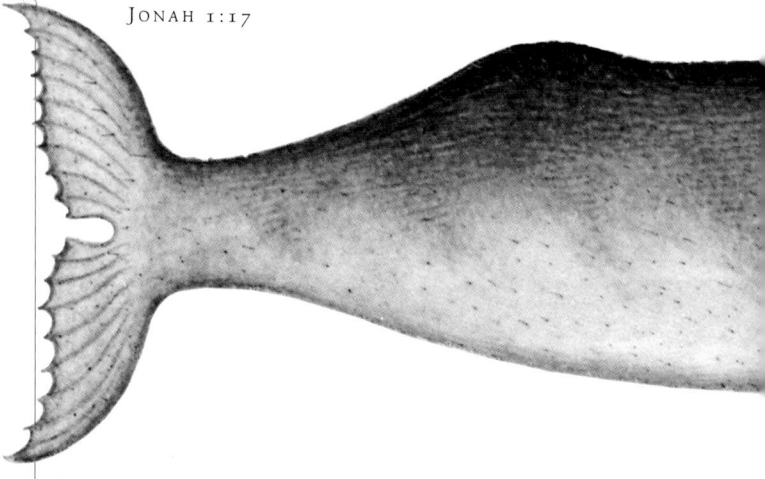

The voice of my beloved! Look, he comes, leaping upon the mountains, bounding over the hills. My beloved is like a gazelle or a young stag. Look, there he stands behind our wall, gazing in at the windows, looking through the lattice.

SONG OF SOLOMON 2:8–9

. . . when a bird flies through the air, no evidence of its passage is found; the light air, lashed by the beat of its pinions and pierced by the force of its rushing flight, is traversed by the movement of its wings, and afterward no sign of its coming is found there . . .

THE WISDOM OF SOLOMON 5:11

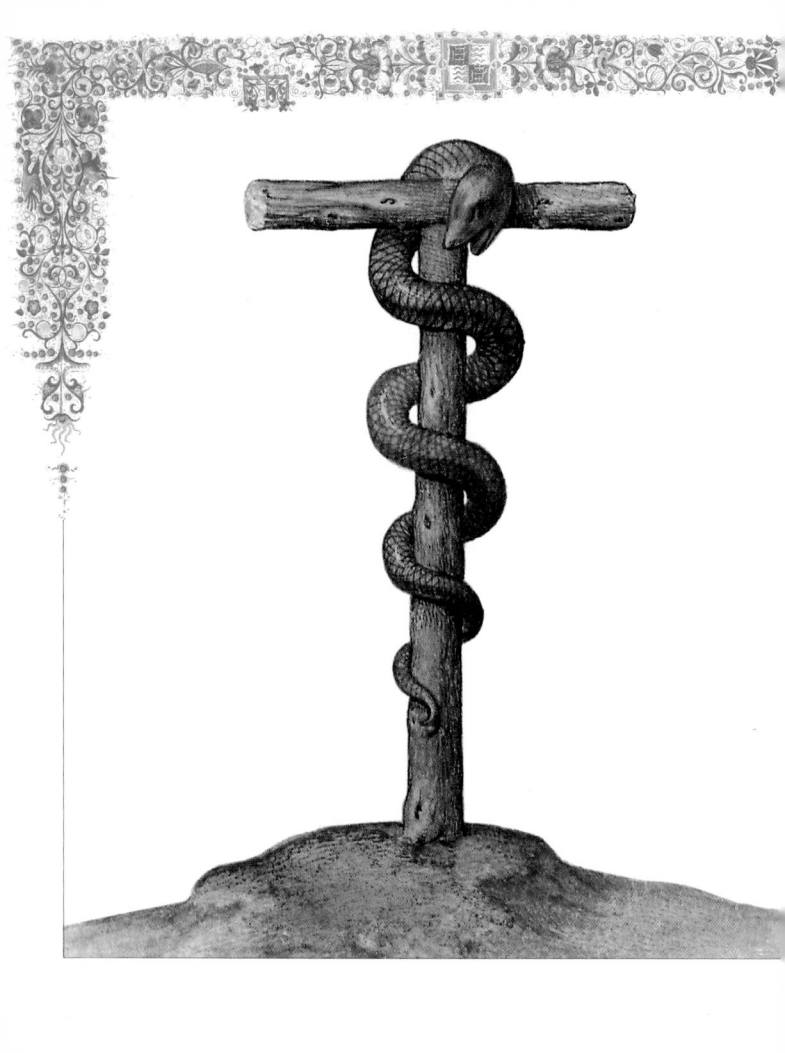

Who pities a snake charmer when he is bitten, or all those who go near wild animals? So no one pities a person who associates with a sinner and becomes involved in the other's sins.

ECCLESIASTICUS 12:13–14

Does a lion roar in the forest, when it has no prey? Does a young lion cry out from its den, if it has caught nothing? Does a bird fall into a snare on the earth, when there is no trap for it? Does a snare spring up from the ground, when it has taken nothing?

AMOS 3:4–5

. . . the lizard can be grasped in the hand, yet it is found in kings' palaces.

PROVERBS 30:28

He was driven from human society, and his mind was made like that of an animal. His dwelling was with the wild asses, he was fed grass like oxen, and his body was bathed with the dew of heaven. . . .

DANIEL 5:21

I am like an owl of the wilderness, like a little owl of the waste places. I lie awake; I am like a lonely bird on the housetop.

PSALMS 102:6–7

For every species of beast and bird, of reptile and sea creature, can be tamed and has been tamed by the human species, but no one can tame the tongue—a restless evil, full of deadly poison.

JAMES 3:7–8

Let the human race lament, but let the wild animals of the field be glad; let all who have been born lament, but let the cattle and the flocks rejoice. It is much better with them than with us; for they do not look for a judgment, and they do not know of any torment or salvation promised to them after death.

2 Esdras 7:65–66

Feasts are made for laughter; wine gladdens life, and money meets every need. Do not curse the king, even in your thoughts, or curse the rich, even in your bedroom; for a bird of the air may carry your voice, or some winged creature tell the matter.

ECCLESIASTES 10:19–20

Deliver my soul from the sword,

my life from the power of the dog!

Save me from the mouth of the

lion! From the horns of the wild oxen you have rescued me.

PSALMS 22:20–21

But a stupid person will get understanding, when a wild ass is born human.

JOB 11:12

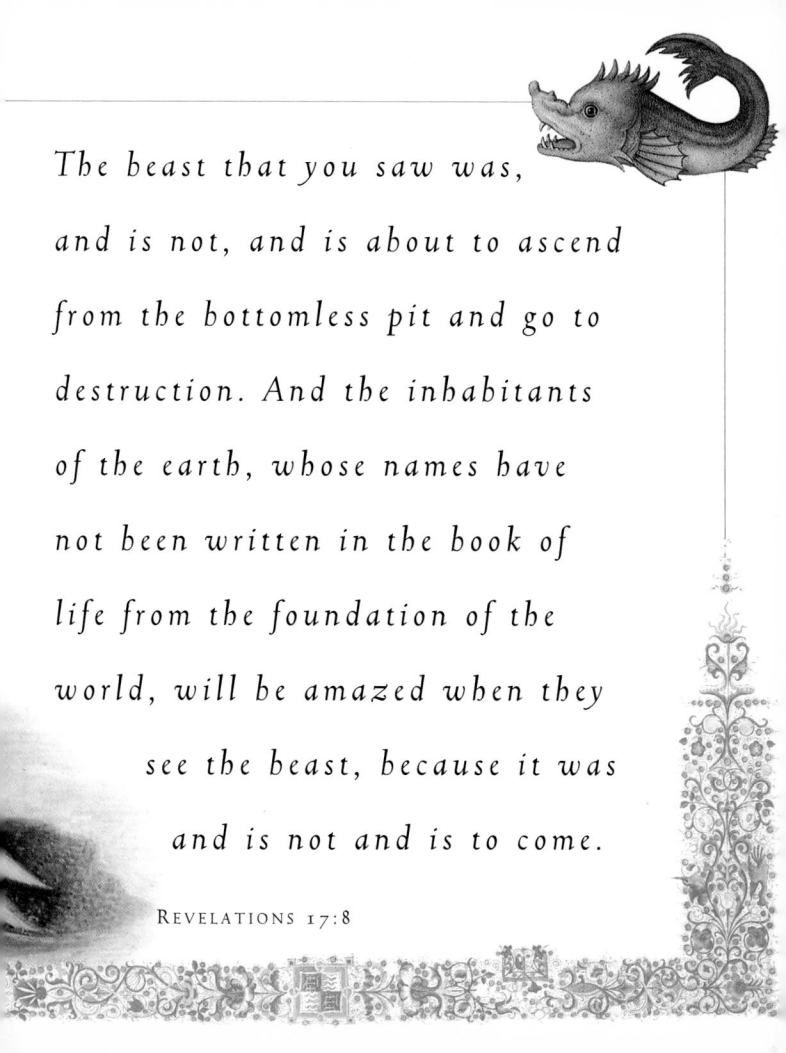

The beast that you saw was, and is not, and is about to ascend from the bottomless pit and go to destruction. And the inhabitants of the earth, whose names have not been written in the book of life from the foundation of the world, will be amazed when they see the beast, because it was and is not and is to come.

REVELATIONS 17:8

What peace is there between a hyena and a dog? And what peace between the rich and the poor?

ECCLESIASTICUS 13:18

A firstborn bull—majesty is his! His horns are the horns of a wild ox; with them he gores the peoples, driving them to the ends of the earth; . . .

DEUTERONOMY 33:17

I looked up and saw a ram standing beside the river. It had two horns. Both horns were long, but one was longer than the other, and the longer one came up second. I saw the ram charging westward and northward and southward. All beasts were powerless to withstand it, and no one could rescue from its power; it did as it pleased and became strong.

DANIEL 8:3–4

Do not deliver the soul of your dove to the wild animals; do not forget the life of your poor forever.

PSALMS 74:19

And the beast that I saw was like a leopard, its feet were like a bear's, and its mouth was like a lion's mouth. . . .

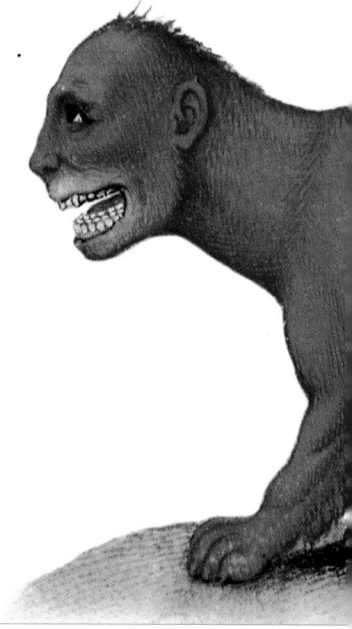

REVELATIONS 13:2

My heart is in anguish within me, the terrors of death have fallen upon me. Fear and trembling come upon me, and horror overwhelms me. And I say, "O that I had wings like a dove! I would fly away and be at rest . . ."

PSALMS 55:4–6

. . .Through a land of trouble and distress, of lioness and roaring lion, of viper and flying serpent, they carry their riches on the backs of donkeys. . . .

ISAIAH 30:6

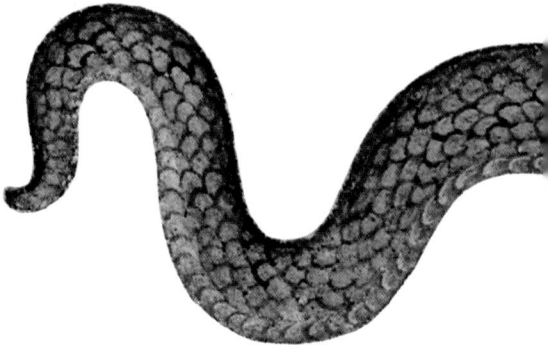

When my soul was embittered, when I was pricked in heart,

I was stupid and ignorant;

I was like a brute beast

toward you.

PSALMS 73:21–22

". . . There is no rest day or night for those who worship the beast and its image and for anyone who receives the mark of its name."

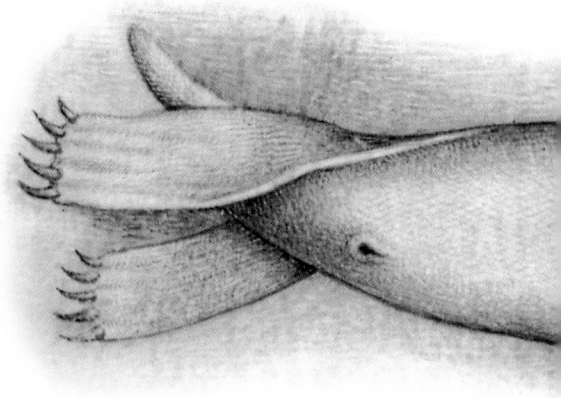

REVELATIONS 14:11

The trees of the Lord are watered abundantly, the cedars of Lebanon that he planted. In them the birds build their nests; the stork has its home in the fir trees. The high mountains are for the wild goats; the rocks are a refuge for the coneys.

PSALMS 104:16–18

I will make for you a covenant on that day with the wild animals, the birds of the air, and the creeping things of the ground; and

I will abolish the bow, the sword, and war from the land; and I will make you lie down in safety.

HOSEA 2:18

Three things are stately in their stride; four are stately in their gait: the lion, which is mightiest among wild animals and does not turn back before any; the strutting rooster, the he-goat, and a king striding before his people.

PROVERBS 30:29–31

I adjure you, O daughters of Jerusalem, by the gazelles or the wild does: do not stir up or awaken love until it is ready!

SONG OF SOLOMON 2:7

The great dragon was thrown down, that ancient serpent, who is called the Devil and Satan, the deceiver of the whole world—he was thrown down to the earth, and his angels were thrown down with him.

REVELATIONS 12:9

. . . and four great beasts came up out of the sea, different from one another. The first was like a lion and had eagles' wings. Then, as I watched, its wings were plucked off, and it was lifted up from the ground and made to stand on two feet like a human being; . . .

DANIEL 7:3–4

And I saw three foul spirits like frogs coming from the mouth of the dragon, from the mouth of the beast, and from the mouth of the false prophet.

REVELATIONS 16:13

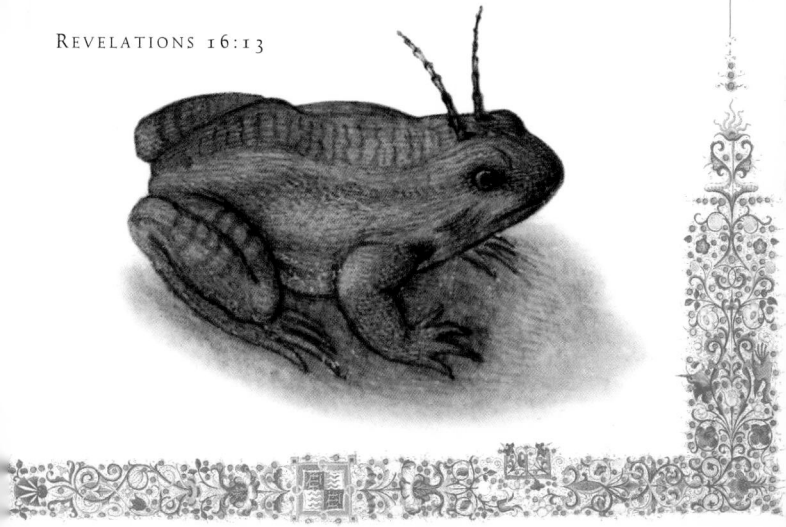

. . . the locusts have no king,

yet all of them march in rank; . . .

PROVERBS 30:27